I see the same stuff each day. The bath, the
fridge, the lampost, the bicycle, the tree...

I've convinced myself that inside each of
these normal, unassuming things there are
hundreds of surprising ideas waiting to be
discovered. I just have to look hard enough
to find them.

This book contains some of the ideas I've
found.

Dominic Wilcox

Dominic
Wilcox
Dec 2012

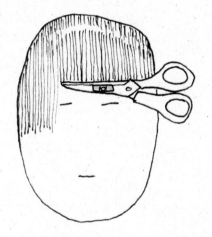

Spirit level for perfectly horizontal haircuts

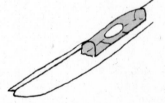

Hair dryer

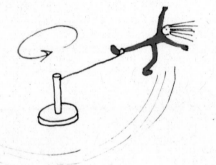

Personal Head Air Bag

Name GPS

For those who forget
names in social situations

→ "You are facing 'Tom'
turn left to face
'Clare'."

Electric

Dodgem Roller Skates

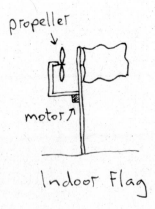

propeller

motor

Indoor Flag

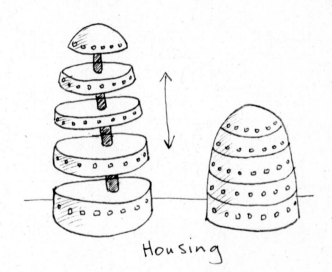

Housing

Family
Bean Bag

Portable Bottom Seat

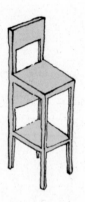

Bunk Chair

Queue Head Rest

cushion

Make use of the person infront
Handy for drinks and snacks

Queue
Shoulder
Hook
Table

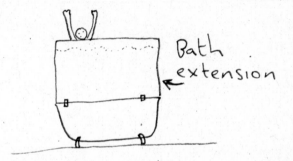

Bath
extension

2nd Brain

Wig with built-in
camera and
microphone to
act as a memory
back-up.

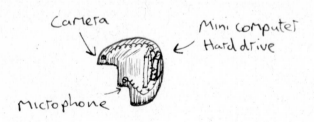

Camera

Mini computer
Hard drive

Microphone

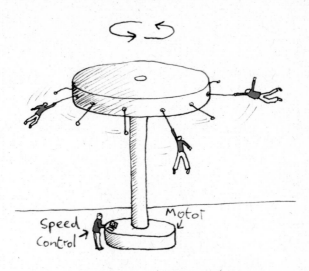

Machine to strengthen
the grip of those with
a weak handshake.

Sideways Trampoline

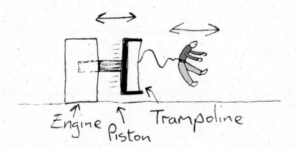

Engine   Piston   Trampoline

Hot air balloon
with side basket

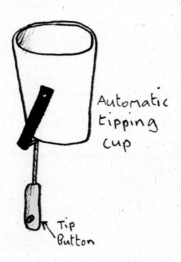

Automatic
tipping
cup

Tip
Button

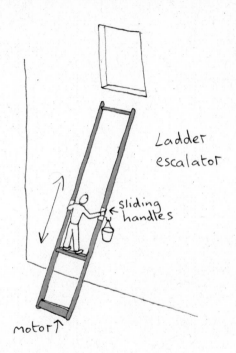

Ladder
escalator

← sliding
handles

motor ↑

Skis made of ice
for street use

Sick Bag Beard

Sick bag →
False beard ←

Be sick without attracting the public's attention.

Man being sick on bus.

Punishment for litterers

Giant Frisbee Transport

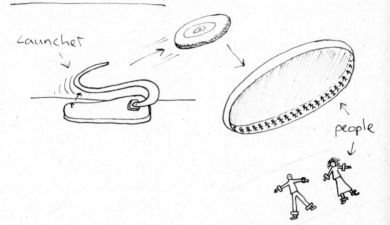

Launcher

people

when the eyes open the eyelashes
hit the bell which rings to indicate
that the sleeping person has woken up.

Genetically modified square peas
to stop rolling around on plate
for easier eating.

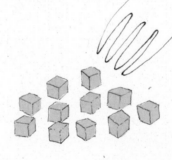

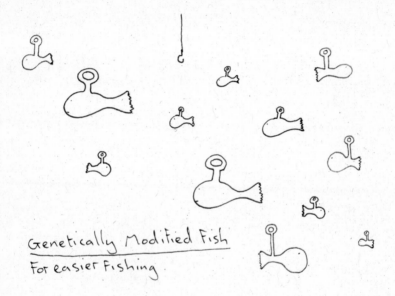

Genetically Modified Fish

For easier Fishing.

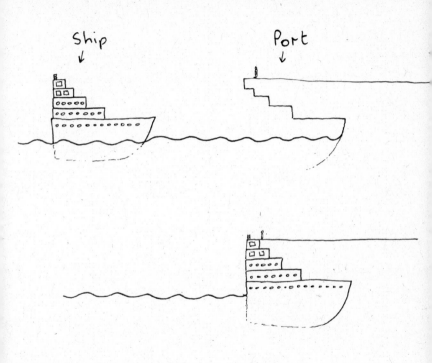

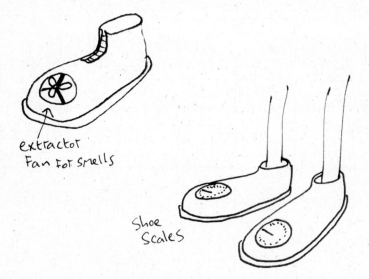

extractor
Fan For Smells

Shoe
Scales

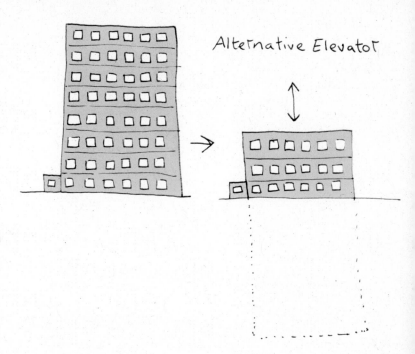

Alternative Elevator

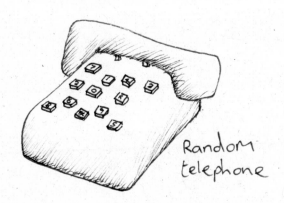

Random
telephone

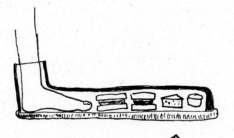

Secret snack area

Eyebrow clip spectacles

Dual use coffin/workdesk

Ideal for those who work hard
all their lives and then die.

Scarf with internal
propeller engine.

Space saving
   Elastic measuring tape

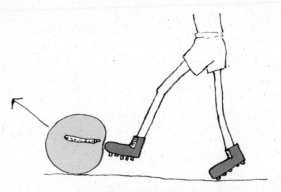

Ball Kick Smoothie Maker

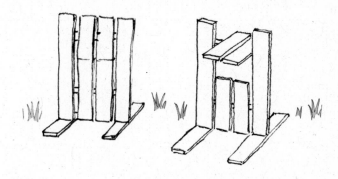

Sitting on the fence seat

Nose Holes to cover

A = 0 1 2
G = 0 1 2 3
C* = 0 2
D* = 2

O = left nostril

Musical Nose Job

Three holes are made
in the nasal passage.

On/off

suction motor

Drinking straw
Suction adapter.
For those who
don't wish to waste
their energy sucking.

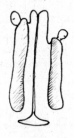

Apparatus for vertical sleeping.

Sleave
Bag

zip>

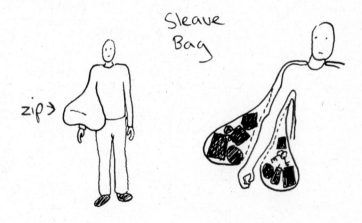

Live Video Dating

For men who find
it easier to talk
to women on an
LCD screen.

Home visitor stats
Sept 2012
TOTAL VISITORS: 54
UNIQUE VISITORS: 19
AVERAGE TIME OF VISIT: 1hr 36 mins
AVERAGE AGE: 27
AVERAGE WEIGHT: 63 KG

A doorbell with visitor stats

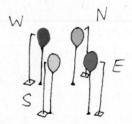

Wind direction device.

A balloon pops on a pin
in the direction the wind
blows, therefore revealing
the wind direction.

Climbing Wall Kitchen Design

For weight loss and healthy living

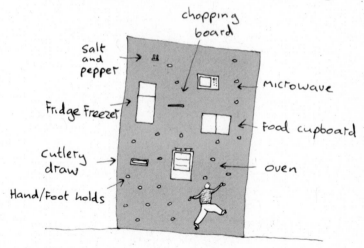

Touchscreen
Nose stylus
Ideal for using
your phone on
cold days while
keeping your gloves on.
Or enabling use of
touchscreen (with unusable
wet hands) in the bath.

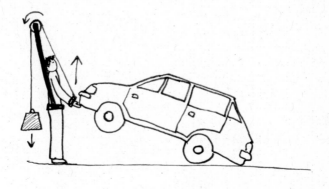

A device to increase arm strength

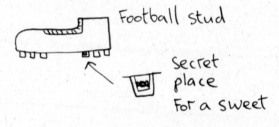

Football stud

Secret
place
for a sweet

Personal Canned Laughter

Makes your terrible jokes seem hilarious

How to appear to make
eye contact whilst also
accurately touching
glasses when toasting
each other.

One way mirror

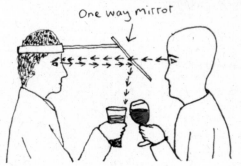

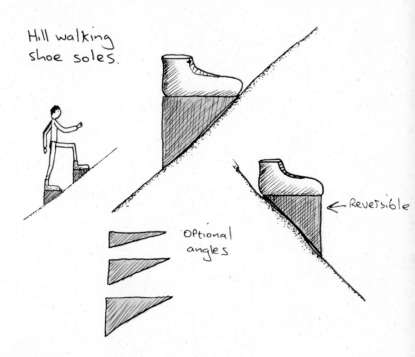

Hill walking shoe soles.

Optional angles

← Reversible

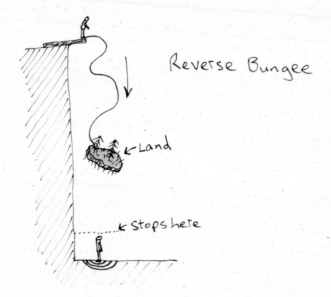

Reverse Bungee

←Land

←stops here

Vote rigging avoidance method

The voters stick their vote directly onto the politician of their choice. Thus the winner is clearly seen.

Lecture accessories

Ringtone detecting
telephone blaster

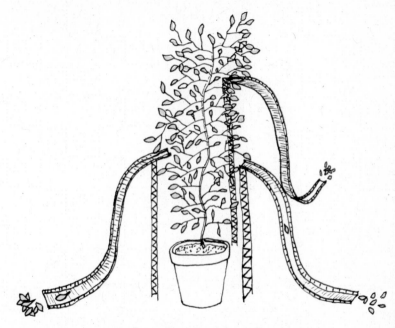

Slides For Falling leaves

vertical queue

Queue Jumper

Punishment for queue jumpers

TV monitor   video camera

Unsubtle device for reading a
fellow passenger's newspaper.

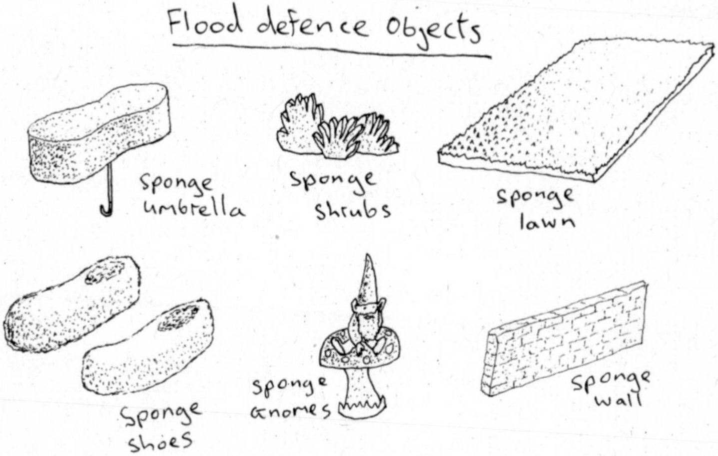

Flood defence objects

Sponge
umbrella

Sponge
shrubs

Sponge
lawn

Sponge
shoes

Sponge
gnomes

Sponge
wall

The 'Hug Bug'

← or →

Drive in either direction while hugging

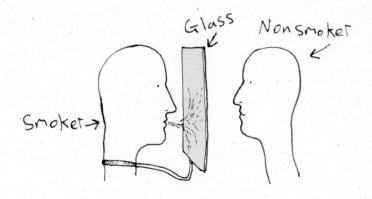

Glass

Nonsmoker

Smoker→

A device to enable non-smokers to talk to smokers.

Spread out while satisfying your partner's need for a cuddle

Soft breath
Simulation

The three stages of relationships

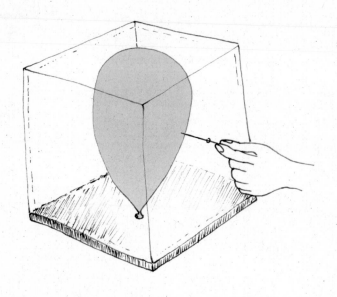

Sound Proof Balloon Popping Box

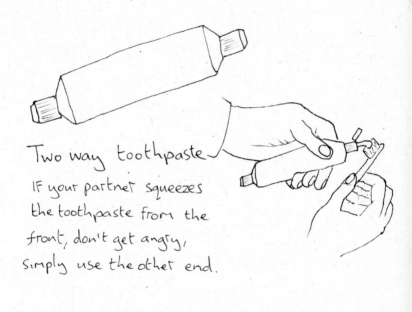

Two way toothpaste

IF your partner squeezes
the toothpaste from the
front, don't get angry,
simply use the other end.

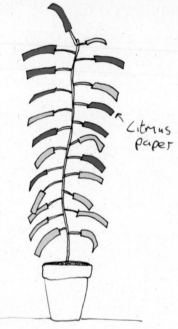

Litmus paper

Beautiful Litmus Plant
Turns a lovely red in acid rain

High rise building disguised as grassy hill.

Disciplining Law Breakers

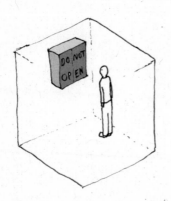

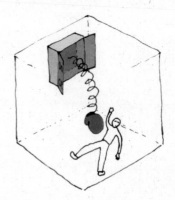

① Place lawbreaker in room   ② wait

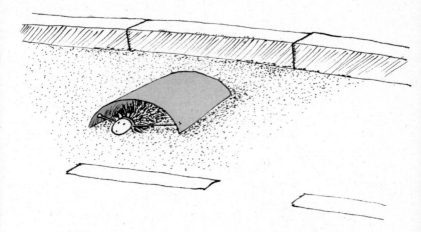

Hedge Hog Road Crossing Protection Device

Smash Avoidance
Beer Bottle Design

impact
sensor

air bag
inflates on
impact

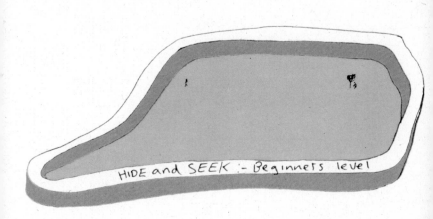

HIDE and SEEK :- Beginners level

Insulting Ball

Encourages youngsters to kick it and therefore improve their skills.

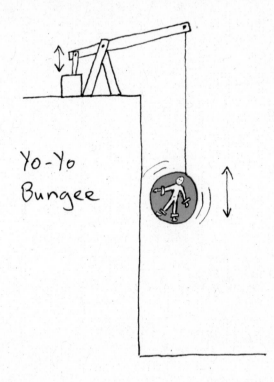

Yo-Yo
Bungee

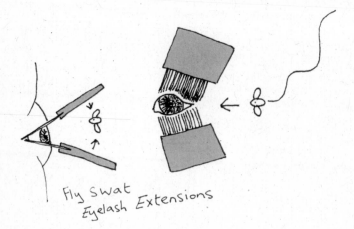

Fly Swat
Eyelash Extensions

WaterFall Umbrella

Family Poncho

A bicycle that loses
weight as you cycle

Avoid getting chocolatey fingers when dunking with these chocolate biscuits with handles

Chocolate

Biscuit handle

salty thumb lolly

Piggy back seat

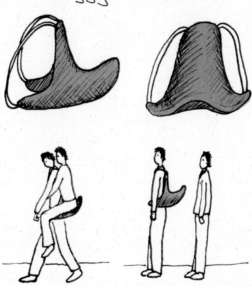

Device to calculate whether a street post can pass between legs without risking injury.

If post height is greater than the inside leg measurement then red light flashes.

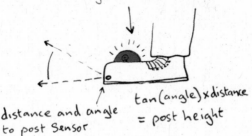

distance and angle to post sensor

tan(angle) × distance = post height

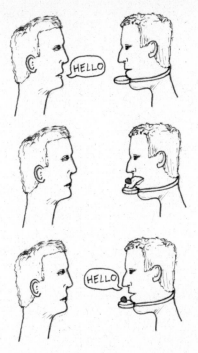

Don't speak with your mouth full.

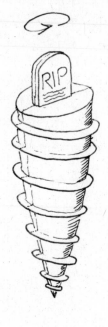

Screw-in coffins

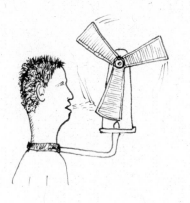

Make use of your sneezing with this wearable ornamental windmill.

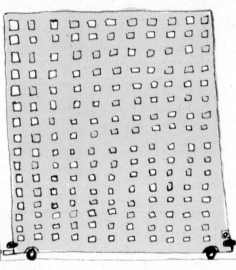

Multi-storey Housing Car

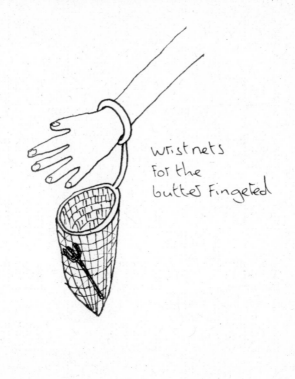

wrist nets
for the
butter fingered

Get away from it all.

For those who wish to go
somewhere and just stick
their head in the ground.

A specially designed head hole
with air pipe.

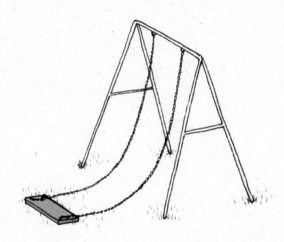

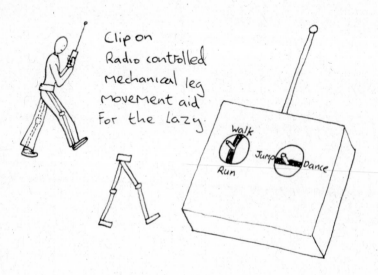

Clip on
Radio controlled
Mechanical leg
movement aid
For the lazy.

Walk
Run
Jump
Dance

Cost Saving 5 plank Fence

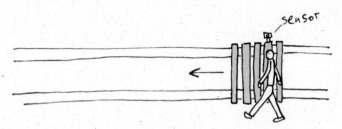

sensor detects position of person
and moves fence accordingly

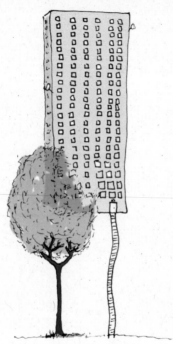

Tree Housing Estate

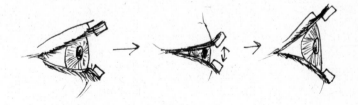

Eyelash attachments
using two repelling magnets
of the same polarity to
stop audience members
falling asleep

Tear off
table cloth

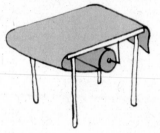

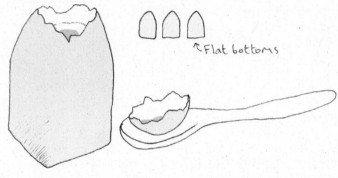

↖ Flat bottoms

Genetically modified egg (cup)

Personal space accessory

note:
Possible issue of
excessive distance
if two people wearing
the device meet.

Bottle attachments to allow more
sophisticated drinking out of the bottle

Dominic Wilcox lives and works in Hackney, London. He makes innovative objects, drawings and installations that have been exhibited worldwide. His diverse work includes miniature sculptures balanced on the hands of watches, a record containing the sounds of people making things and a performance at London's V&A museum where he raced against a 3D Printer to make a model of St Paul's Cathedral from marzipan.

Website: www.dominicwilcox.com
Blog: www.variationsonnormal.com
Twitter: @dominicwilcox

ISBN 978-1-909093-09-6